NEW JERSEY

The Garden State

BY
JOHN HAMILTON

Abdo & Daughters

An imprint of Abdo Publishing | abdopublishing.com

abdopublishing.com

Published by ABDO Publishing, a division of ABDO, PO Box 398166, Minneapolis, Minnesota 55439. Copyright © 2017 by Abdo Consulting Group, Inc. International copyrights reserved in all countries. No part of this book may be reproduced in any form without written permission from the publisher. ABDO & Daughters™ is a trademark and logo of ABDO Publishing.

Printed in the United States of America, North Mankato, Minnesota.
042016
092016

THIS BOOK CONTAINS
RECYCLED MATERIALS

Editor: Sue Hamilton   **Contributing Editor:** Bridget O'Brien
Graphic Design: Sue Hamilton
Cover Art Direction: Candice Keimig   **Cover Photo Selection:** Neil Klinepier
Cover Photo: iStock
Interior Images: Alamy, AP, Comstock, Corbis, Getty, Granger, Gunter Kuchler, History in Full Color-Restoration/Colorization, iStock, John Hamilton, Library of Congress, Mars, Inc., Mile High Maps, Minden Pictures, NASA, New Jersey Devils, New York Public Library, One Mile Up, Science Source, Time and Valleys Museum, Trenton Historical Society, and Wikipedia.

Statistics: *State and City Populations*, U.S. Census Bureau, July 1, 2015/2014 estimates; *Land and Water Area*, U.S. Census Bureau, 2010 Census, MAF/TIGER database; *State Temperature Extremes*, NOAA National Climatic Data Center; *Climatology and Average Annual Precipitation*, NOAA National Climatic Data Center, 1980-2015 statewide averages; *State Highest and Lowest Points*, NOAA National Geodetic Survey.

Websites: To learn more about the United States, visit booklinks.abdopublishing.com. These links are routinely monitored and updated to provide the most current information available.

Cataloging-in-Publication Data

Names: Hamilton, John, 1959- author.
Title: New Jersey / by John Hamilton.
Description: Minneapolis, MN : Abdo Publishing, [2017] | Series: The United
    States of America | Includes index.
Identifiers: LCCN 2015957622 | ISBN 9781680783322 (lib. bdg.) |
    ISBN 9781680774368 (ebook)
Subjects: LCSH: New Jersey--Juvenile literature.
Classification: DDC 974.9--dc23
LC record available at http://lccn.loc.gov/2015957622

CONTENTS

THE GARDEN STATE

New Jersey is a state with a rich history and many natural resources. It is also a land of contrasts and contradictions. New Jersey is the fourth-smallest state, but one of the most heavily populated. Much of the state is covered by cities and roadways. It is sandwiched between the major metropolitan areas of New York City, New York, and Philadelphia, Pennsylvania. However, there is also much natural beauty, which surprises many visitors. There are quiet forests, secluded back roads, and many miles of sandy beaches facing the Atlantic Ocean.

During its colonial days, farmers made good use of New Jersey's rich soil. Today, farmland covers approximately 15 percent of the state's land area. Bountiful harvests of tomatoes, peppers, spinach, and blueberries feed not only New Jersey citizens, but also neighboring states. That is why New Jersey is nicknamed "The Garden State," as a reminder of its agricultural roots.

A field of sunflowers on a farm in The Garden State.

Construction began on the Red Mill in Clinton, New Jersey, in 1810. Over time, it was used to grind everything from flour and feed to graphite and talc. Today, it is a museum.

QUICK FACTS

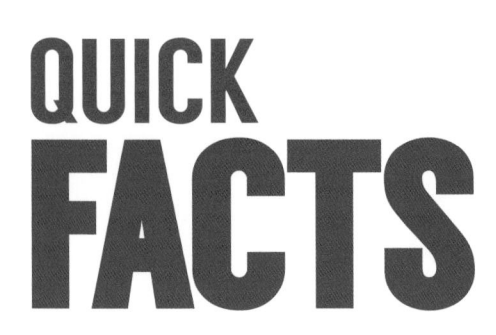

Name: New Jersey is named after the island of Jersey, the largest of the Channel Islands in the English Channel.

State Capital: Trenton, population 84,034

Date of Statehood: December 18, 1787 (3rd state)

Population: 8,958,013 (11th-most populous state)

Area (Total Land and Water): 8,723 square miles (22,592 sq km), 47th-largest state

Largest City: Newark, population 280,579

Nickname: The Garden State

Motto: Liberty and Prosperity

State Bird: Eastern Goldfinch

State Flower: Violet

State Tree: Red Oak

State Bug: Honeybee

State Fruit: Blueberry

Highest Point: High Point, 1,803 feet (550 m)

Lowest Point: Atlantic Ocean, 0 feet (0 m)

Average July High Temperature: 85°F (29°C)

Record High Temperature: 110°F (43°C), in Runyon on July 10, 1936

Average January Low Temperature: 22°F (-6°C)

Record Low Temperature: -34°F (-37°C), in River Vale on January 5, 1904

Average Annual Precipitation: 47 inches (119 cm)

Number of U.S. Senators: 2

Number of U.S. Representatives: 12

U.S. Presidents Born in New Jersey: Stephen Grover Cleveland (1837-1908)

U.S. Postal Service Abbreviation: NJ

QUICK FACTS

GEOGRAPHY

New Jersey is the fourth-smallest state in the United States. Its land and water area is just 8,723 square miles (22,592 sq km). Despite its small size, there are many kinds of terrain in New Jersey. There are tall mountains, rolling hills, marshes, beaches, and rivers.

To the north and northeast of New Jersey is the state of New York. The lower two-thirds of eastern New Jersey borders the Atlantic Ocean. To the southwest of the state is northern Delaware. New Jersey's long western border is separated from Pennsylvania by the Delaware River.

New Jersey's Mount Tammany is the southernmost peak of the Kittatinny Mountains. Across the Delaware River is the state of Pennsylvania.

High Point

NEW YORK

CONNECTICUT

KITTATINNY MTS

Hudson River

Paterson

Jersey City

Newark

Elizabeth

Trenton

PENNSYLVANIA

Delaware River

NEW JERSEY

ATLANTIC OCEAN

N

0   50 miles
0   50 km

Atlantic City

DELAWARE

New Jersey's total land and water area is 8,723 square miles (22,592 sq km). It is the 47th-largest state. The state capital is Trenton.

New Jersey has four main geographic regions. They include the Valley and Ridge, Highlands, Piedmont, and Coastal Plain regions.

The Valley and Ridge region is in the northwest corner of New Jersey. It is home to the Kittatinny Mountains (also called Kittatinny Ridge). They are part of the Appalachian Mountains. There are steep mountain ridges and valleys. New Jersey's highest spot is in this region. It is called High Point. It stands 1,803 feet (550 m) tall.

East of the Valley and Ridge region is the Highlands region. It is hilly and rocky, with many lakes.

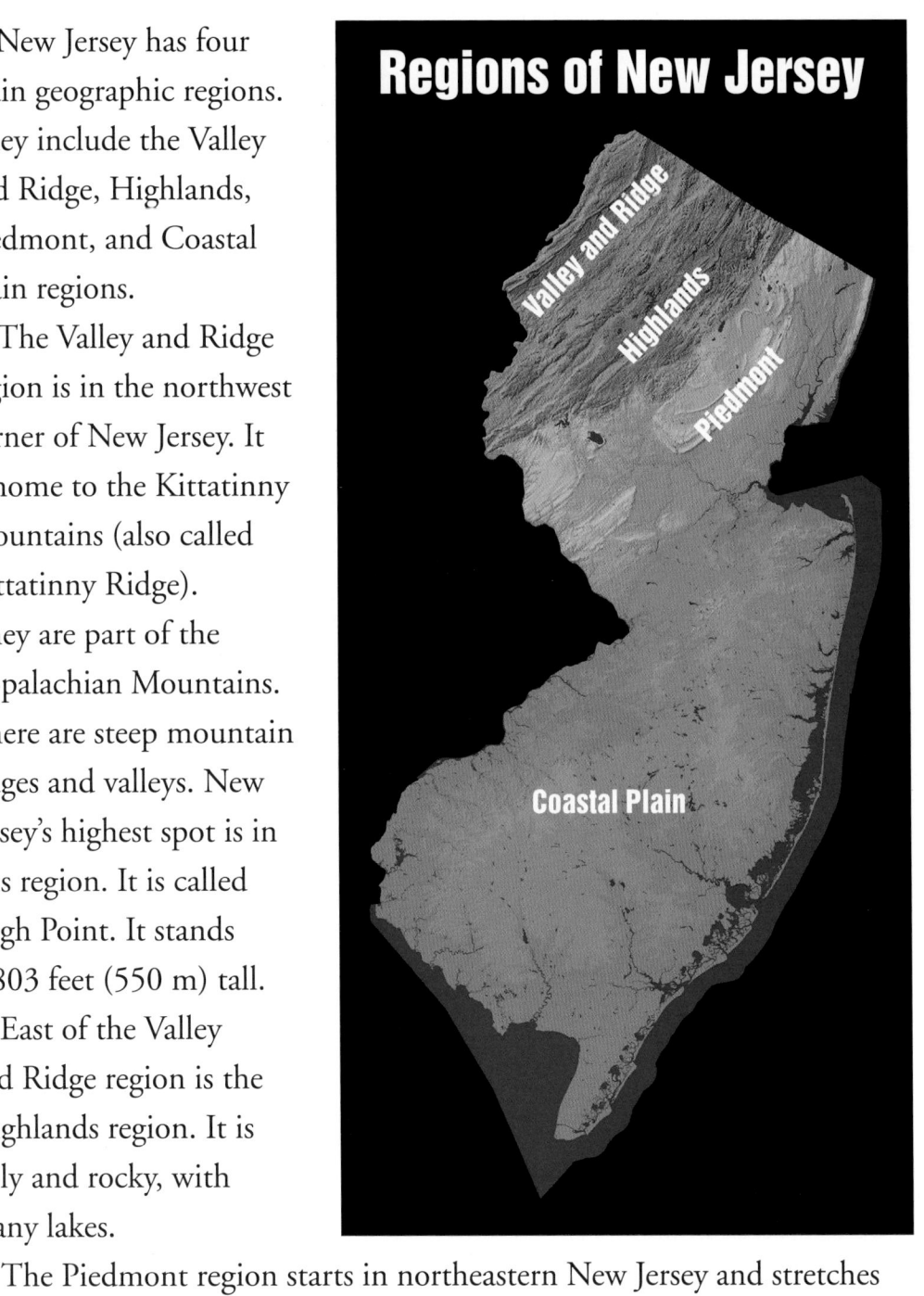

Regions of New Jersey

Valley and Ridge

Highlands

Piedmont

Coastal Plain

The Piedmont region starts in northeastern New Jersey and stretches across the state to the southwest. There is level land and rolling hills. Most of New Jersey's large, industrial cities are located in the Piedmont.

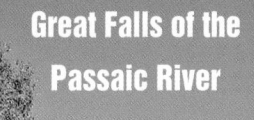

Great Falls of the Passaic River

The Great Falls of the Passaic River are in the Piedmont region, in the city of Paterson. The falls are 77 feet (23 m) high. The swift water powered textile mills in the 1800s. Today, the beautiful landmark is a major tourist attraction.

The Palisades are also in the Piedmont. They are a series of steep cliffs, about 300 feet (91 m) high, that stretch for 20 miles (32 km) along the Hudson River in northeastern New Jersey.

The Coastal Plain region occupies the southern three-fifths of New Jersey. There are many pine forests. Parts of the flat land are good for farming. There are many sandy beaches and barrier islands along the Atlantic Ocean coastline.

GEOGRAPHY

CLIMATE AND WEATHER

Most of New Jersey has a humid subtropical climate. It is warmer in the southern areas. Summers are warm and humid, while winters are cool but not harsh. Statewide, the average July high temperature is 85°F (29°C). In January, the average low temperature is 22°F (-6°C). The hottest temperature ever recorded in New Jersey happened on July 10, 1936, in the town of Runyon. That day, the thermometer rose to a sweltering 110°F (43°C).

Because of higher altitudes, it is cooler in the mountainous northwestern part of the state. Even in northeastern New Jersey, where altitudes are lower, it can sometimes get quite cold in winter. In the town of River Vale, on January 5, 1904, the thermometer sank to -34°F (-37°C), a state record. The climate along New Jersey's Atlantic Ocean coast is usually mild, thanks to steady ocean temperatures.

Jersey City, New Jersey, gets hit with a heavy winter snowstorm in 2016. Winters are usually cool, but not harsh, in the state.

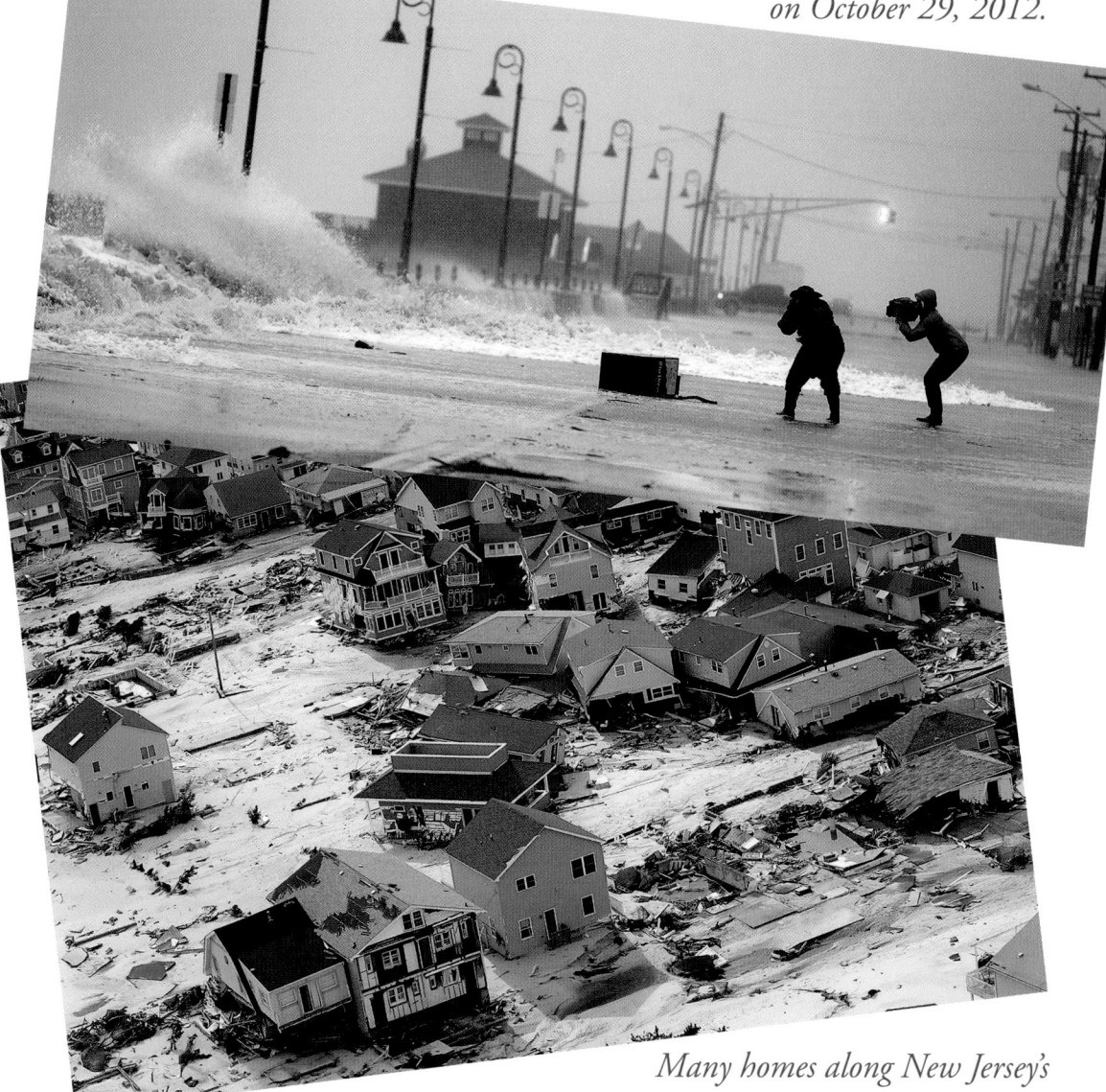

A news crew films Hurricane Sandy's approach on October 29, 2012.

Many homes along New Jersey's coast were destroyed by Hurricane Sandy.

New Jersey usually gets plenty of rain. It averages 47 inches (119 cm) of precipitation each year. Severe weather is rare, but can be deadly. Coastal storms called nor'easters often strike in autumn and winter. They can cause damaging winds and flooding. In 2012, Hurricane Sandy flooded several coastal cities and caused 43 deaths.

PLANTS AND ANIMALS

About 2 million acres (809,371 ha) of New Jersey is covered by forestland. That is about one-third of the state. Most of the forestland is in small patches measuring less than 1,000 acres (405 ha). The official state tree is the red oak. It is found throughout New Jersey. In the north, common tree species include oak, hickory, maple, birch, ash, and hemlock. The southern forests are dominated by white cedar, oak, and pine.

New Jersey's official state flower is the violet. These delicate, purple flowers are found in New Jersey fields and meadows. Other common wildflowers found in the state include azaleas, buttercups, coneflowers, daisies, lady's slippers, and Queen Anne's lace. In the bogs of southern New Jersey are carnivorous plants that eat insects. They include pitcher plants, Venus flytraps, and sundews.

Pine Barrens Tree Frog

Goldfinch On Coneflower

Sundew With A Captured Moth

New Jersey's
Pine Barrens is also called
"Pinelands," or just "The Pines."

New Jersey is home to a large forest called the Pine Barrens. It has sandy soil that is poor for farming, but supports dense forests of pine and oak. Hundreds of species of mammals, birds, amphibians, and reptiles are sheltered in the Pine Barrens. Many are endangered, including the rare Pine Barrens tree frog.

15

Even though New Jersey is small and densely populated, it is home to a wide variety of wildlife. That is because the state has so many kinds of habitats, including woodlands, fields, meadows, and seashores.

White-tailed deer and black bears are found throughout the state. Other common mammals found in New Jersey include red and grey foxes, muskrats, coyotes, groundhogs, beavers, otters, raccoons, skunks, opossums, and rabbits.

Raccoons

Great Egret

New Jersey is an important resting stop for birds following the spring and fall migrations along the East Coast. Bald eagles are sometimes sighted in wooded areas. White and blue herons gather in New Jersey's wetlands. Other common birds include cardinals, wild turkeys, egrets, and woodpeckers. The eastern goldfinch is New Jersey's official state bird.

There are at least 36 species of frogs, salamanders, and toads that live in the wetlands of New Jersey. Some bullfrogs grow more than 6 inches (15 cm) long. The eastern tiger salamander, New Jersey's largest amphibian, measures 8 inches (20 cm) long.

Dozens of species of snakes, turtles, and lizards make their home in New Jersey. Snapping turtles, which can grow to over 20 inches (51 cm), are found throughout the state. Two venomous snakes are found in New Jersey: the northern copperhead and the timber rattlesnake.

Fish swimming in New Jersey's freshwater lakes and streams include largemouth bass, pickerel, sunfish, and catfish. Saltwater fish off the Atlantic Ocean coast include sea bass, flounder, cod, and bluefish.

PLANTS AND ANIMALS

HISTORY

People first came to the New Jersey area about 10,000 years ago. These Paleo-Indians were the ancestors of today's Native Americans. They were nomads who hunted large herd animals such as caribou and mastodons.

By the 1500s, Native American people had settled in the New Jersey area. They called themselves the Lenni Lenape, which means "original people." Since many of their villages were near the Delaware River, Europeans called them the Delaware people.

Paleo-Indians were the ancestors of today's Native Americans. They hunted large herd animals such as mastodons and caribou.

Giovanni da Verrazzano

The first European to visit New Jersey was Italian explorer Giovanni da Verrazzano. He arrived by ship in 1524. Eighty-five years later, in 1609, English explorer Henry Hudson sailed up a large river bordering northeastern New Jersey. Today, that river is called the Hudson River. Henry Hudson was working for a Dutch company. He claimed all the land around the Hudson River for the Dutch, including a part of modern New Jersey. The Dutch called the territory New Netherland. Dutch and Swedish settlers soon arrived.

In 1664, England took control of New Netherland during a war with the Dutch. The English renamed it New Jersey, after the island of Jersey, the largest of the Channel Islands in the English Channel.

Over the next 100 years, many settlers came to New Jersey, hoping for land to farm, and for freedom of religion. The Lenni Lenape Native Americans were angry when the newcomers cleared forestland to make room for farms and industry. Many Lenni Lenape moved away to Pennsylvania or New York. Others died from diseases that the European colonists brought with them, such as smallpox and measles. Eventually, most of the Lenni Lenape disappeared from New Jersey.

During the mid-1700s, New Jersey colonists grew angry over the many English laws and taxes they felt were harsh and unfair. Some wanted independence from Great Britain. Many others wanted to remain British citizens. They were called Tories. Finally, in 1776, New Jersey joined the other 12 American colonies and declared independence.

General Washington crosses the Delaware River during the Revolutionary War.

During the Revolutionary War (1775-1783), New Jersey found itself between two major cities. Philadelphia, Pennsylvania was to the west, while New York City, New York, was to the east. Because of this, both American and British armies often clashed in New Jersey. It was the site of more than 100 battles. New Jersey was nicknamed the "Crossroads of the Revolution." Important battles in New Jersey included the Battle of Trenton, the Battle of Princeton, and the Battle of Monmouth. At the Battle of Trenton, General George Washington famously crossed the frozen Delaware River and defeated a stronghold of Hessian troops, which helped turn the tide of the war.

After the Revolutionary War, on December 18, 1787, New Jersey ratified, or approved, the United States Constitution. New Jersey became the third state to join the Union. The city of Trenton became the state capital in 1790. William Livingston was the first governor.

During the early 1800s, cities and factories sprang up as the industrial revolution swept the country. Roads, canals, and railroads helped spur new industries.

During the Civil War (1861-1865), New Jersey fought for the Union against the Southern Confederacy. More than 25,000 New Jersey soldiers fought against slavery and to keep the United States from breaking up.

After the Civil War, New Jersey's factories continued to grow. The state's population boomed. New Jersey resident Thomas Alva Edison invented many new products that changed the way Americans lived. At his research labs in Newark, Menlo Park, and West Orange, he and his coworkers invented devices such as electric lighting and phonographs.

Thomas Edison was known as the New Jersey Wizard of Menlo Park.

In 1913, New Jersey Governor Woodrow Wilson became the 28th president of the United States.

New Jersey's population doubled between 1900 and 1930. However, when the Great Depression of the 1930s struck, the state suffered greatly. Businesses went bankrupt, and many people lost their jobs. After World War II (1939-1945), New Jersey began to bounce back, led by the state's large electrical and chemical industries.

Today, New Jersey's cities continue to grow. The state is making progress in tackling problems such as traffic, housing, crime, and equal rights. It is expanding and diversifying its economy, especially the tourism industry, so that New Jersey can better handle future challenges.

ATLANTIC CITY
The Playground of the World

DID YOU KNOW?

Peregrine Falcon

• The Delaware Water Gap is in the mountainous northwestern side of New Jersey, along the border of Pennsylvania. It is a spot where, over millions of years, the Delaware River has carved a gorge through the surrounding mountain ridge. The Delaware Gap National Recreation Area is popular with boaters, hikers, and rock climbers. Bird watchers enjoy spotting peregrine falcons that nest in the forests of the mountain slopes.

• The Jersey Devil is a mythical beast that haunts the forests of the Pine Barrens in southern New Jersey. Storytellers say the creature stands upright, has cloven hooves like a horse, giant bat-like wings, clawed hands, and the head of a goat. Stories of the Jersey Devil have been told for hundreds of years. The National Hockey League's New Jersey Devils are named after the beast.

• M&M's candy was invented in New Jersey. Forrest Mars Sr., of the Mars Company, was in Europe in the 1930s during the Spanish Civil War. He saw soldiers eating a British candy called Smarties, which had chocolate encased in a hard candy shell that prevented the chocolate from melting. In 1941, Mars invented his own process for making the candy and patented it. It was an immediate hit. The company's Newark, New Jersey, factory made M&M's by the millions. Today, it is the most popular candy in the world.

• One of the busiest bridges in the country is the George Washington Bridge. It is a suspension bridge that spans the Hudson River, connecting New Jersey with northern Manhattan, New York. Opening to traffic in 1931, it is the fourth-largest suspension bridge in the United States. It has two levels and 14 lanes of traffic that handle about 300,000 vehicles daily. The bridge is 4,760 feet (1,451 m) long. It is supported by four main cables that are suspended between two 570-foot (174-m) steel towers. The cables are 3 feet (.9 m) in diameter. Each cable itself is a bundle of 434 individual wires.

DID YOU KNOW?

PEOPLE

Stephen Grover Cleveland (1837-1908) was the 22nd *and* the 24th president of the United States. A Democrat, he served from 1885-1889 and from 1893-1897. He is the only president to serve two non-consecutive terms. Cleveland was born in Caldwell, New Jersey, and spent his early childhood in the state. He worked as a teenager to support his poor family. He later studied law and went into politics. As president, he was a reformer who tried to stop corruption in government and big corporations. He was praised for being honest, fair, and independent. However, during his second term, the economy suffered a severe downturn. He left office very unpopular, although historians have later been more kind in judging his presidency. After leaving the White House, Cleveland went back to New Jersey to retire.

Edwin "Buzz" Aldrin (1930-) is a former NASA astronaut, United States Air Force jet pilot, and engineer. He was the pilot of the Apollo 11 lunar module *Eagle*. On July 20, 1969, he became the second person to walk on the Moon (a few minutes after mission commander Neil Armstrong). Before the Apollo mission, he first went into space in 1966 piloting the spacecraft for Gemini 12. He performed three spacewalks totaling 5.5 hours, a record at the time. After his NASA career, he became the commander of the United States Air Force Test Pilot School at California's Edwards Air Force Base. After retirement, he became an author and a promoter of space exploration. Aldrin was born in Glen Ridge, New Jersey, and grew up in nearby Montclair.

Bruce Springsteen (1949-) is an American rock legend. Nicknamed "The Boss," he is a talented singer, songwriter, and musician. He was born in Long Branch, New Jersey, and grew up in Freehold. His lyrics are often about ordinary working-class people and their struggles. His career began in the 1960s when he performed in music clubs in New Jersey beach towns such as Asbury Park. With his E Street Band and as a solo musician, he has sold millions of records worldwide. His biggest albums include 1975's *Born to Run* and 1984's *Born in the U.S.A.* He has won 20 Grammy Awards for his music. In 1999, Springsteen was inducted into the Rock and Roll Hall of Fame.

Dorothea Lange (right) was known for her photo of a migrant mother (below).

Dorothea Lange (1895-1965) was one of the most important photojournalists of the 20th century. During the Great Depression of the 1930s, she worked for the United States government's Farm Security Administration. She documented the plight of the rural poor, the unemployed, and the homeless. Her intimate portraits showed people's humanity in the face of hard times. Lange was born in Hoboken, New Jersey.

Shaquille O'Neal (1972-) is a former star player of the National Basketball Association (NBA). After a stellar college career playing for Louisiana State University, O'Neal went pro in 1992, playing for the Orlando Magic, where he earned Rookie of the Year honors. During his long NBA career, he also played for the Los Angeles Lakers, Miami Heat, Phoenix Suns, Cleveland Cavaliers, and Boston Celtics. He was named league MVP in 2000, and won four NBA championships. O'Neal was born in Newark, New Jersey.

PEOPLE

CITIES

Trenton has been the capital of New Jersey since 1790. Located in the west-central part of the state, its population is approximately 84,034. Originally settled by a religious group called the Quakers, the city was named after merchant William Trent, who helped develop the area in the early 1700s. For a brief time in 1784, after the Revolutionary War, Trenton was temporarily the capital of the United States. Once a center of manufacturing, today the city's biggest employer is state government. The New Jersey State Museum includes exhibits on Native Americans, fine art, and New Jersey history. Just north of Trenton is Washington Crossing State Park, where General George Washington famously crossed the icy waters of the Delaware River.

Newark is the largest city in New Jersey. Its population is approximately 280,579. Once an industrial powerhouse, today the city's economy depends more on banking, insurance, and law firms. Health care and government are also big employers. Newark is a major transportation hub that includes a large airport, train stations, and a busy shipping port. The city is home to many performing arts organizations and museums. The New Jersey Symphony Orchestra and New Jersey State Opera are both housed at the New Jersey Performing Arts Center in downtown Newark. The state's largest museum is the Newark Museum. It houses works of fine art from all around the world, natural history exhibits, and a planetarium.

Jersey City is the second-largest city in New Jersey. Its population is approximately 262,146. It is in northeastern New Jersey, across the Hudson River from New York City, New York. It is home to a busy seaport, several shopping districts, and financial services companies. Liberty State Park, along the waterfront, has spectacular views of New York City and Liberty Island, home of the Statue of Liberty.

Paterson is New Jersey's third-largest city. Its population is about 146,753. It is named after William Paterson, who was the second governor of the state, from 1790 to 1793, and an associate justice of the United States Supreme Court. Paterson is nicknamed "The Silk City" because its factories made so much silk cloth in the late 1800s. Today, the city's factories produce chemicals and electronic equipment. The landmark Great Falls of the Passaic River are in the city.

Atlantic City is a resort town along the Atlantic Ocean coast. It is famous for its casinos and its boardwalk along the sandy Jersey Shore. Its population is approximately 39,415. Atlantic City is on Absecon Island, just off the mainland. There are many hotels, shops, restaurants, and museums. Saltwater taffy was invented in Atlantic City in the late 1800s. Many of the properties in the board game Monopoly are named after streets in Atlantic City.

The city of **Elizabeth** is home to approximately 128,705 people. It is New Jersey's fourth-largest city. Founded in 1665, it was the first English-speaking community in New Jersey. Today, its train stations, airport, and busy seaport make the city an important transportation center for the East Coast. Elizabeth is a very diverse city, with residents representing more than 50 countries and 37 languages.

TRANSPORTATION

New Jersey has been a crossroads of the East Coast since colonial times. Today, many people travel through the state on their way to big cities like New York City, New York, or Philadelphia, Pennsylvania. There are 39,293 miles (63,236 km) of public roadways in New Jersey. The most famous roadway in the state is the New Jersey Turnpike. It carries vehicle traffic between Delaware and New York. Another important road is the Garden State Parkway. It stretches across New Jersey from north to south, and connects New York City with Atlantic City.

Ferries carry passengers between
New Jersey and New York.

New Jersey has 17 freight railroads that haul heavy cargo on 981 miles (1,579 km) of track across the state. The most common products carried by train include chemicals, food products, paper, refined petroleum products, motor vehicle parts, and cargo containers. New Jersey also has a large network of commuter rail service that crisscrosses the state.

People in New Jersey have long used the state's waterways to transport goods from place to place. Today, there are many ferryboats that whisk commuters to jobs in neighboring states.

Newark Liberty International Airport is one of the country's busiest airports, handling up to 37.5 million passengers yearly. Several other airports serve the state, including Atlantic City International Airport and Trenton-Mercer Airport.

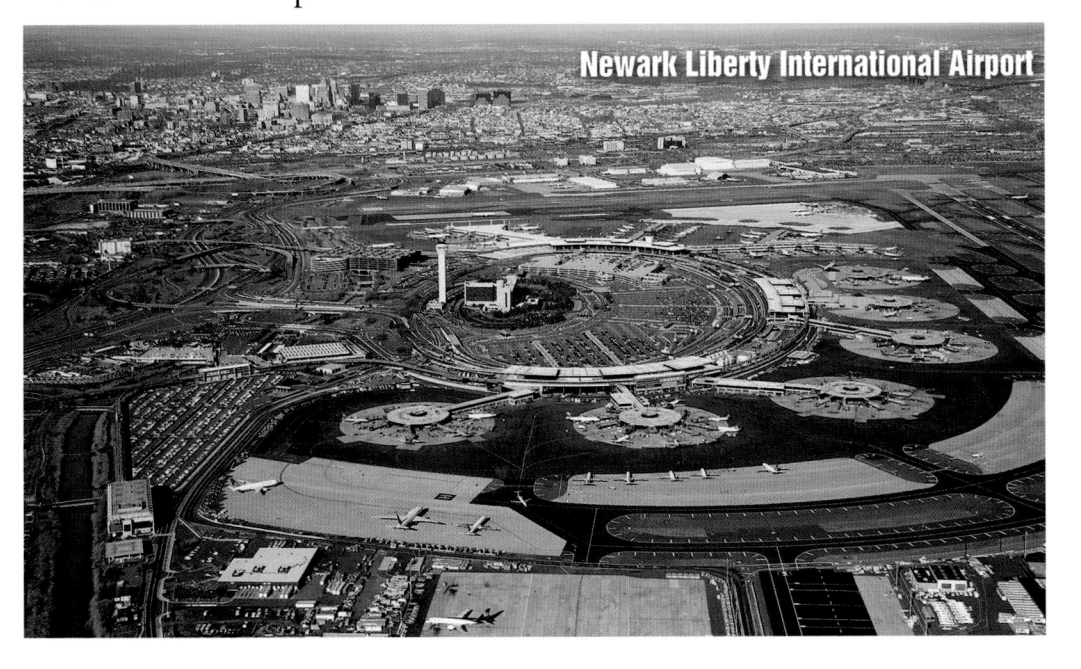

Newark Liberty International Airport

TRANSPORTATION

NATURAL
RESOURCES

Approximately 15 percent of New Jersey's land area is farmland. That is about 4.7 million acres (1.9 million ha) of land. There are about 9,100 farms in the state, with an average size of 79 acres (32 ha).

The most valuable crops grown in The Garden State include corn to feed livestock, sweet corn, bell peppers, hay, and soybeans. Farmers in New Jersey also grow cucumbers, tomatoes, cranberries, peaches, cabbage, spinach, squash, sweet potatoes, wheat, beans, blueberries, eggplants, and lettuce. Decorative flowers, dairy products, and horses are also profitable farm products.

A cranberry harvest in New Jersey.

A fishing boat passes the Barnegat Lighthouse off Long Beach Island in Ocean County, New Jersey. The state has six major commercial fishing ports.

New Jersey has six major commercial fishing ports along its lengthy Atlantic Ocean coast. Cape May, on the very southern tip of the state, is the largest and most active. The most economically important seafood catches include sea scallops, surf clams, Atlantic mackerel, blue crabs, fluke, monkfish, Atlantic herring, and lobsters.

Several kinds of raw materials are dug from beneath New Jersey's crust. They include crushed stone, clay, industrial sand, plus sand and gravel. Peat and greensand are used as fertilizers.

NATURAL RESOURCES

INDUSTRY

New Jersey's workforce totals about 4.5 million people. Most are employed in the service industry. Instead of manufacturing products, service industries sell services to businesses and consumers. The biggest service industry companies in New Jersey are banking and insurance. Other businesses include commercial real estate, advertising, education, health care, restaurants, retail stores, law, marketing, and tourism.

Manufacturing is not the powerhouse industry it once was in New Jersey. However, many important products are still made that greatly add to the state's economy. New Jersey is a leading state for manufacturing chemicals. Some are used to make medicines. Large pharmaceutical companies in New Jersey include Johnson & Johnson and Merck. Other products that use New Jersey chemicals include shampoos, detergents, paints, and plastics.

Merck is one of the largest pharmaceutical companies in the world. Its United States headquarters is in Kenilworth, New Jersey.

Food processing is another leading manufacturing item. It includes products such as canned fruits and vegetables, roasted coffee, bakery products, beverages, and candies. Mars, the maker of M&M's, Snickers, and Twix, has a large manufacturing plant in Hackettstown, New Jersey.

New Jersey is also a big manufacturer of electronic products used in computers and communications equipment. Tyco International is a large security systems maker with its company headquarters in Princeton, New Jersey.

Tourism is another big industry in New Jersey, especially in Atlantic City and other resort destinations along the Jersey Shore. Tourism brings millions of visitors to the state each year.

SPORTS

The New Jersey Devils skate in the National Hockey League. Based in Newark, they have won three Stanley Cup championships.

Two National Football League teams from neighboring New York play their home games at MetLife Stadium in East Rutherford, New Jersey. The teams include the New York Giants and the New York Jets. The Giants have won the Super Bowl four times, while the Jets have won once. MetLife Stadium is one of the most expensive stadiums ever built, at a cost of $1.6 billion. It is part of the vast Meadowlands Sports Complex.

The New York Red Bulls are a Major League Soccer team. They play home games at Red Bull Arena in Harrison, New Jersey.

High school and college sports are closely followed in The Garden State. One of the biggest college rivalries is between Rutgers University and Princeton University. Seton Hall University's basketball team is usually a powerhouse contender.

Thoroughbred horse racing and harness racing are popular sports in New Jersey. Major tracks include the Meadowlands Racetrack in East Rutherford, the Freehold Raceway in Freehold, and Monmouth Park Racetrack in Oceanport.

American Pharoah, ridden by Victor Espinoza, wins The William Hill Haskell Invitational at Monmouth Park Racetrack in 2015.

There are many activities for outdoor lovers in New Jersey. Hikers and joggers enjoy the many miles of beaches along the Jersey Shore. Delaware Water Gap in northwestern New Jersey is a popular place for canoeing. Mountain Creek is one of the biggest ski resorts on the East Coast.

Thousands of people enjoy the beach along the Jersey Shore.

ENTERTAINMENT

Many popular musicians and performers can be seen in New Jersey's nightclubs and concert halls. New Jersey native and megastar Bruce Springsteen got his start playing in small clubs along the Jersey Shore. Other famous musicians from New Jersey include Frank Sinatra, Sarah Vaughan, Queen Latifah, and the rock group Bon Jovi.

Lucy the Elephant is a famous New Jersey landmark. It is in Margate City, just south of Atlantic City, along the Jersey Shore. The 60-foot (18-m) -long wooden pachyderm was built in 1881. It has served as a cottage, an office, and a restaurant. Today, it is a National Historic Landmark.

Lucy the Elephant was constructed in 1881 by James Lafferty. He used her to help sell real estate and bring tourists to Margate City.

WORLD'S LARGEST ELEPHANT

Tourists enjoy the famous Atlantic City Boardwalk. Some visitors travel along the Boardwalk in rolling chairs. First introduced during a convention in 1887, they remain a fun way to see the area.

Near Trenton, history buffs can witness reenactments of General George Washington crossing the Delaware River. At the nearby Old Barracks Museum, visitors can experience the lives of Revolutionary War soldiers. They can also learn how military doctors worked.

There are many museums and art galleries in New Jersey. The Zimmerli Art Museum, at Rutgers University in New Brunswick, has 60,000 works of fine art. It is famous for it collections of French, Russian, and American art.

For many visitors, no trip to New Jersey is complete without a stroll along the famous Atlantic City Boardwalk. First opened in 1870, the walkway runs along the beach for several miles, passing stores, nightclubs, arcades, restaurants, and museums.

ENTERTAINMENT

TIMELINE

8000 BC—The first Paleo-Indians venture into the New Jersey area.

1500s—Lenni Lenape Native Americans settle into villages, many along the Delaware River.

1524—Explorer Giovanni da Verrazzano is the first European to see present-day New Jersey.

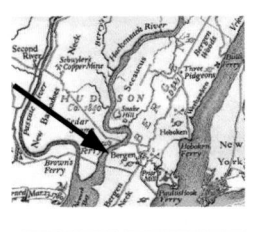

1609—Explorer Henry Hudson sails up the Hudson River and claims the New Jersey area for the Dutch. The Dutch call the new territory New Netherland.

1660—The village of Bergen is established. It becomes New Jersey's first town. Today it is called Jersey City.

1664—England takes control of the area. They rename it New Jersey.

1774—A shipment of British tea is burned by angry colonists in Greenwich. The event is called the Greenwich Tea Party.

1776—New Jersey joins the other 12 American colonies in declaring independence from Great Britain.

1787—New Jersey becomes the third state in the Union.

1790—Trenton becomes the state capital of New Jersey.

1876—Thomas Edison opens a research and development lab in Menlo Park.

1931—The George Washington Bridge, the world's only 14-lane bridge, opens.

1976—Casino gambling for Atlantic City is legalized, revitalizing the city.

1994-2001—Christine Todd Whitman takes office as New Jersey's first woman governor.

2012—Hurricane Sandy ravages the New Jersey coast, including the Atlantic City area. Thousands of citizens are forced to evacuate. The storm kills 43 people in New Jersey and causes approximately $37 billion in damage.

2016—The Seton Hall Pirates men's college basketball team wins the Big East Conference championship and makes its 10th appearance at the NCAA Men's Division I Basketball Tournament.

GLOSSARY

COMMUTE

Travel between a person's work and home.

GORGE

A narrow cleft with steep, rocky walls, like a small canyon.

HESSIANS

Professional soldiers from several regions of today's Germany, who were paid to fight for the British military. Americans often referred to any German soldier as a "Hessian." About 30,000 Hessians served in North America during the American Revolution. The British wanted them because the soldiers had a reputation for being skilled and ruthless in battle. Thousands of Hessians, however, deserted and fought for the Americans. There were also many Americans of German decent who fought in the war.

INDUSTRIAL REVOLUTION

A period of time, starting in the late 1700s, when machines began taking over many types of work that previously had been done by hand.

MASTODON

An extinct mammal that lived long ago. It resembled a large elephant. Remains of the creature have been found all over the world.

NOR'EASTER

A large storm that forms when warm air over the Atlantic Ocean clashes with cold Arctic air blown in from Canada. Nor'easters get their name from the northeasterly direction of their winds. They can be very destructive, but are usually less dangerous than tropical hurricanes.

PHONOGRAPH

A device that plays sounds and music. Sound vibrations are recorded as tiny grooves on the surface of a rotating cylinder or disk. To play back the sounds, a small stylus, or needle, moves across the grooves. Its vibrations are amplified by a loudspeaker, which reproduces the original sound or music.

QUAKER

A member of the Religious Society of Friends. It is a Christian group that was founded in 1650 by George Fox.

SPECIES

A class of plants or animals that are very similar.

SUSPENSION BRIDGE

A bridge with its deck supported by large cables hung from towers.

TELEGRAPH

A machine that sends electronic signals representing letters of the alphabet and numbers across great distances along a wire. The message itself is also known as a telegraph.

TORIES

Colonists who remained loyal to England during the American Revolutionary War (1775-1783).

TROPICAL STORM

A storm with winds between 39 and 73 mph (63 and 117 kph). Tropical storms can create significant rainfall. Their winds can cause beach erosion and damage coastal structures. Tropical storms sometimes strengthen to become hurricanes.

INDEX